EXPLORING THE Arctic

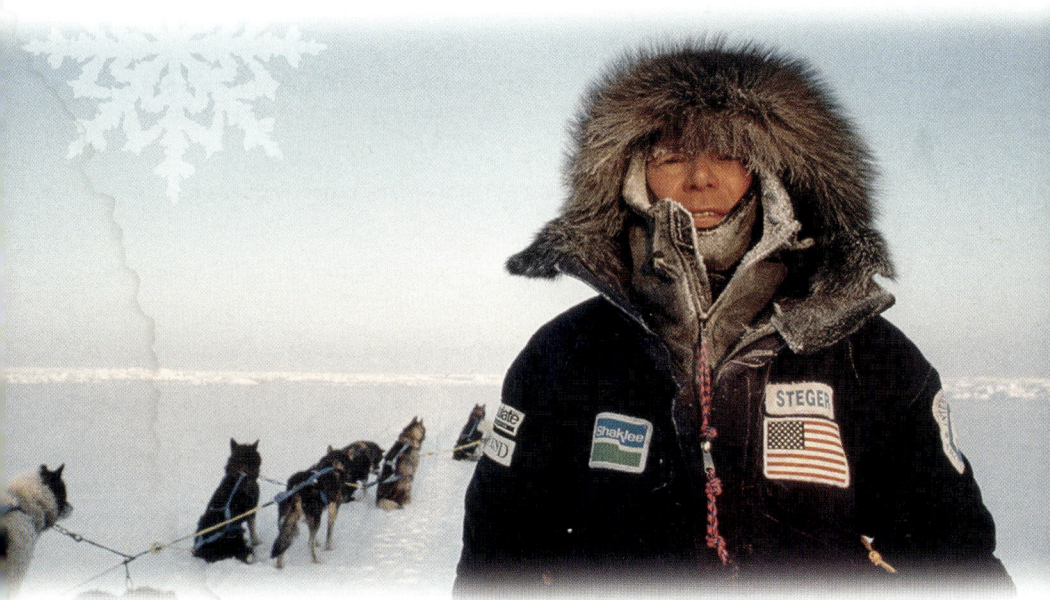

by Linda Cernak

Scott Foresman
is an imprint of
PEARSON

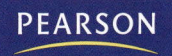

Glenview, Illinois • Boston, Massachusetts • Chandler, Arizona •
Upper Saddle River, New Jersey

Photographs

Every effort has been made to secure permission and provide appropriate credit for photographic material. The publisher deeply regrets any omission and pledges to correct errors called to its attention in subsequent editions.

Unless otherwise acknowledged, all photographs are the property of Pearson Education, Inc.

Photo locators denoted as follows: Top (T), Center (C), Bottom (B), Left (L), Right (R), Background (Bkgd)

Opener: ©H. Mark Weidman Photography/Alamy Images; **1** ©Gordon Wiltsie/National Geographic/Getty Images; **3** ©Barrie Watts/©DK Images; **4** ©H. Mark Weidman Photography/Alamy Images; **5** ©Luciano Corbella/©DK Images; **6** Radius Images/Jupiter Images; **7** ©Robert Harding Picture Library Ltd/Alamy Images; **8** (Bkgd) ©Sue Flood/Stone/Getty Images; 9 (Inset) Keystone/Hulton Archive/Getty Images; **10** ©Robert E. Peary/National Geographic/Getty Images; **11** Bettmann/Corbis; **12** (R) Bettmann/Corbis, (L) CORBIS/Corbis; **13** (R) ©Photoshot Holdings Ltd/Alamy Images, (L) Bettmann/Corbis; **14** ©Gordon Wiltsie/National Geographic/Getty Images; **15** AP Images/©AP Photo; **16** Corbis/Jupiter Images.

ISBN 13: 978-0-328-47287-1
ISBN 10:   0-328-47287-5

Copyright © by Pearson Education, Inc., or its affiliates. All rights reserved. Printed in the United States of America. This publication is protected by copyright, and permission should be obtained from the publisher prior to any prohibited reproduction, storage in a retrieval system, or transmission in any form or by any means, electronic, mechanical, photocopying, recording, or likewise. For information regarding permissions, write to Pearson Curriculum Rights & Permissions, One Lake Street, Upper Saddle River, New Jersey 07458.

Pearson® is a trademark, in the U.S. and/or in other countries, of Pearson plc or its affiliates.
Scott Foresman® is a trademark, in the U.S. and/or in other countries, of Pearson Education, Inc., or its affiliates.

4 5 6 7 8 9 10 V010 13

The Arctic is the land and water north of the Arctic Circle, which surrounds the North Pole.

Imagine air so cold that bare fingers freeze in minutes, even seconds. Imagine miles of almost nothing but ice. In the winter, there is barely any daytime, just long hours of darkness. This is the Arctic.

Long ago, native people such as the Inuit were the only humans to have ever seen the Arctic. But explorers have sailed the frigid waters near the North Pole for more than 2,300 years.

The Inuit are one group of native Arctic people.

Parts of North America, Greenland, Europe, and Asia form the coast of the Arctic Ocean. A thick frozen polar ice cap covers the middle part of the ocean. Underneath, the water is very deep.

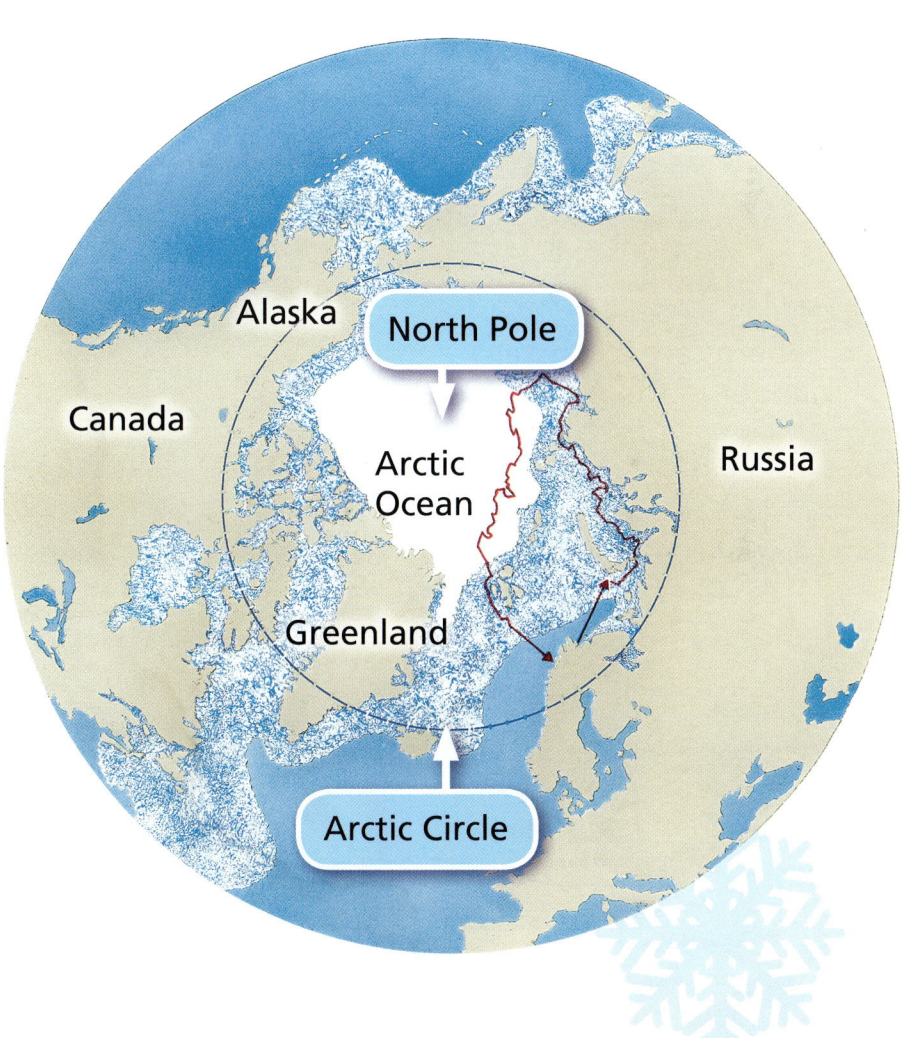

5

The first explorers had no idea how to survive in the Arctic. They brought few supplies. They didn't understand how to live with ice and cold the way the Inuit did. Many of them died.

Icebergs are a constant danger in the Arctic Ocean.

In 1893 the Norwegian explorer Fridtjof Nansen sailed into the Arctic Ocean. His ship, *The Fram*, drifted alongside solid ice. Finding it too hard to navigate through the ice, Nansen and a group of men ended up abandoning the ship. They tried to reach the North Pole by dogsled.

Nansen never reached the North Pole. But he paved the way for other explorers.
In the early 1900s, other explorers raced to be the first to reach the North Pole.

On March 1, 1909, two Americans named Robert Peary and Matthew Henson started off for the North Pole. With them were 23 men, 19 sleds, and a team of 133 dogs. For one month, they traveled north over the Arctic ice.

Peary and his team in front of a flag in the Arctic ice.

As the explorers traveled, small teams of men went ahead. These teams built shelters for the explorers and their supplies.

In the end, only Peary, Henson, and four Inuit men reached the North Pole.

Frederick Cook never did reach the North Pole.

Another American explorer named Dr. Frederick A. Cook claimed to have reached the North Pole in April of 1908—one year before Peary and Henson.

Cook's claim proved to be false, however.

Today people are still unsure if Peary actually stood on the true North Pole. But modern explorers still come to the Arctic. Some of them fly. Some use dogsleds. Some come in submarines!

1926
Richard Byrd flies a plane over the Arctic Circle.

1926
Roald Amundsen flies an airship over the North Pole.

Large ships called icebreakers have hulls made of steel. The steel allows the ship to crush the ice, which, in turn, allows the ship to move forward.

1958

The first submarine sails under the Arctic ice.

1977

The first icebreaker ship reaches the North Pole.

13

Even today, people explore the polar ice cap on foot. They pull their supplies on dogsleds. They face many of the same dangers the early explorers did.

Dangers Explorers Face in the Arctic

- falling through the ice
- frostbite
- getting lost
- blizzards
- running out of food
- injuries to humans or dogsled team

In 1986 Will Steger became the first person to cross the Arctic by dogsled.

In 2007 Barbara Hillary became the first African American woman to reach the North Pole. She was 75 years old!

How do explorers stay warm in the Arctic today? They dress in layers of clothing that protect them against frostbite. Goggles protect their eyes from the harsh glare of the sun on the ice.

Many of today's explorers are tourists. They come on boats to observe wildlife and take pictures. The Arctic is still one of the most challenging places to explore on Earth.

Tourists observe Arctic wildlife such as polar bears, seals, and whales.